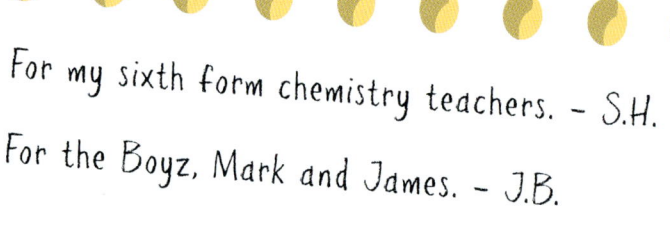

For my sixth form chemistry teachers. – S.H.
For the Boyz, Mark and James. – J.B.

First published in Great Britain 2026 by Red Shed, part of Farshore
An imprint of HarperCollins*Publishers*
1 London Bridge Street,
London SE1 9GF
www.farshore.co.uk

HarperCollins*Publishers*
Macken House, 39/40 Mayor Street Upper
Dublin 1, D01 C9W8, Ireland

Red Shed is a registered trademark of HarperCollins*Publishers* Ltd.

Text copyright © Swapna Haddow 2026
Illustrations copyright © Jess Bradley 2026
Swapna Haddow and Jess Bradley have asserted their moral rights.
Consultancy by Jules Pottle.

ISBN 978 0 00 871336 2
Printed in Malaysia.
1

A CIP catalogue record for this title is available from the British Library.

All rights reserved. No part of this publication may be reproduced, stored in a retrieval system, or transmitted, in any form or by any means, electronic, mechanical, photocopying, recording or otherwise, without the prior permission of the publisher and copyright owner.

Without limiting the exclusive rights of any author, contributor or the publisher of this publication, any unauthorised use of this publication to train generative artificial intelligence (AI) technologies is expressly prohibited. HarperCollins also exercise their rights under Article 4(3) of the Digital Single Market Directive 2019/790 and expressly reserve this publication from the text and data mining exception.

Stay safe online. Any website addresses listed in this book are correct at the time of going to print. However, Farshore is not responsible for content hosted by third parties. Please be aware that online content can be subject to change and websites can contain content that is unsuitable for children. We advise that all children are supervised when using the internet.

Experiments and activities are performed at your own risk, follow the instructions and ALWAYS ask an adult for help. HarperCollins is not responsible for the results of your experiments. Always ask an adult for help with any craft activity or DIY project. Wear protective clothes and cover surfaces to avoid damage or staining.

This book contains FSC™ certified paper and other controlled sources to ensure responsible forest management.

For more information visit: www.harpercollins.co.uk/green

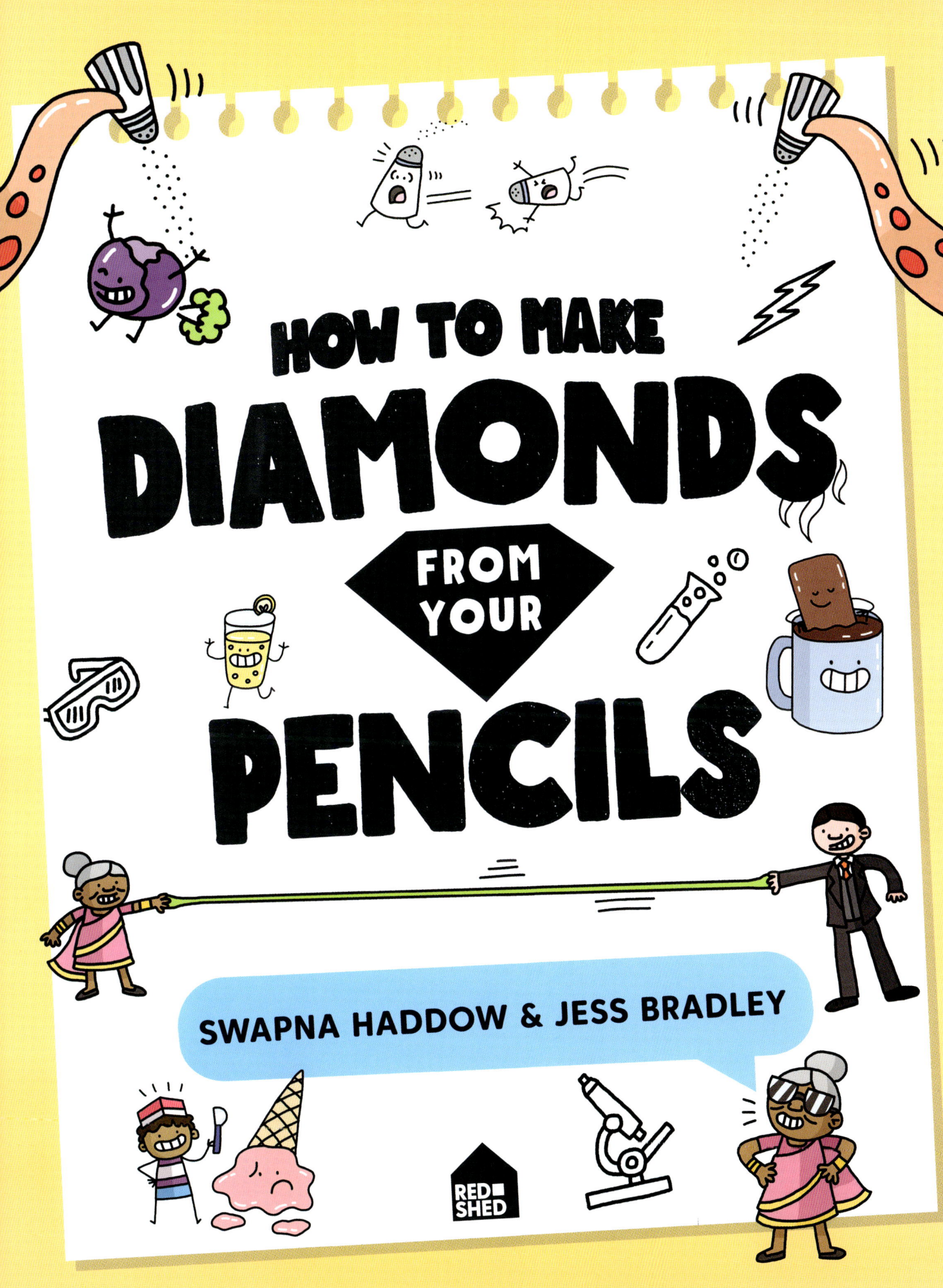

INTRODUCTION

The bonkers world of science has some of the answers to how things work and why things don't. In this book, you will find some ridiculous and not-so-ridiculous dilemmas, which all have solutions from the astonishing and unbelievable world of science. All the hard work has been done for you - thanks to fabulous scientists - but you can test out the science for yourself with an experiment at the end of each section.

You'll come away with all the knowledge you need to tackle all sorts of things - from surviving at sea as a new pirate to carrying a dinosaur egg across a jungle!

And you'll see how making 'mistakes' in science can lead to incredible inventions! That's what happened when US chemist Stephanie Kwolek was working on a project and accidently invented Kevlar - a super strong, lightweight material used in products such as bulletproof vests.

Pssst!

The brilliant thing about science is that even if it doesn't go the way you expect, you've still learned something. You've learned that it doesn't work. The magic of learning through science is that it is all about experimenting and discovering. **JUST MAKE SURE THAT YOU'VE CHECKED WITH A PARENT OR GUARDIAN BEFORE YOU START!** (They can also help with any tricky bits AND you can wow them with your new knowledge!)

CONTENTS

HOW TO . . .
SAVE FIREWORKS NIGHT 8

MAKE DIAMONDS FROM
YOUR PENCILS 12

SURVIVE AT SEA AS
A NEW PIRATE 16

GET CABBAGE OFF
THE SCHOOL MENU 20

MAKE THE MAGIC
SHOW SPARKLE 24

RESCUE YOUR
FRIEND'S PARTY 28

GET ACROSS QUICKSAND 32

CARRY A DINOSAUR EGG
ACROSS A JUNGLE 36

WIN THE SCIENCE FAIR 40

SEND A SECRET
MESSAGE 44

WIN A SCHOOL
COMPETITION 48

BE A DETECTIVE 52

MAKE YOUR OWN
ICE-CREAM STAND 56

GLOSSARY 60

INDEX 61

CALAMITY COMICS

HOW TO SAVE FIREWORKS NIGHT

1

THE SCIENCE COMIC YOU NEVER KNEW YOU NEEDED — CHEMISTRY EDITION

Uh oh, it's fireworks night but nobody brought the fireworks! The entire neighbourhood is standing in a big, freezing-cold field, all the hot dogs have been eaten, and Granny is giving Amy big pleading Granny-eyes . . .

Amy doesn't want to let Granny down . . .

But at this time of night, there isn't a single fireworks shop open.

Quick, Amy needs to entertain the crowd . . .

Especially as everyone is looking a bit cold and a bit annoyed . . .

What do YOU think Amy should do . . .

A) GRAB A CLOTH, METAL SPOON AND A PLASTIC PIPE?

B) TELL EVERYONE TO STAR GAZE?

C) ASK MO TO GIVE A DRONE SHOW?

Turn the book upside down to see the answers!

If you chose **A**, BRILLIANT IDEA! Amy can create sparks with them.

If you chose **B**, oh dear. Granny doesn't take the news well and throws a full Granny tantrum.

If you chose **C**, this goes terribly. Mo crashes the drone in a tree and everyone leaves disappointed.

WHAT'S THE SCIENCE?

Static electricity is going to help Amy create sparks: nature's fireworks! But first, you need to know about **atoms**. Everything, everywhere - you, this book, a dog, the air - is made up of building blocks called atoms. Atoms are so tiny you need a special microscope to see them. They are made up of even tinier particles called **neutrons**, **protons** and **electrons**.

When the surfaces of two objects come together, electrons can jump from one surface to another, creating static electricity. If enough static electricity builds up, it can create sparks.

Want to see this in action? Let's give it a go! Just like ancient Greek philosopher Thales did in around 600BCE when he rubbed amber with wool and it attracted feathers.

MAKE STATIC ELECTRICITY

Have a go at seeing electrons in action as you create static electricity with a balloon.

Static electricity is useful in real life too. For example, it makes plastic food wrap stick to things, helps laser printers work and is how cloths can clean without using chemicals.

You will need:

- Paper
- A hole punch (or use scissors to make small pieces)*
- A balloon

*Be careful - ask an adult for help.

Instructions:

1. Create about 30 small pieces of paper with the hole punch or scissors.

2. Blow up the balloon and tie the end in a knot. You may need an adult to help.

3. Rub the balloon on your head (make sure your hair is clean and dry) or on a woolly jumper or on a football shirt. This will pick up electrons.

4. Hold the balloon close to the paper circles, without touching them. Do they jump to the balloon? If not, rub your hair or clothes again and have another go.

Pssst! To have a go at creating tiny 'fireworks' of your own, rub a balloon on your hair, on a woolly jumper or on a football shirt in a very dark room. Then slowly bring a metal spoon towards the balloon to see a spark jump across.

So, if Amy asked everyone to rub a huge plastic pipe - one that runs from one end of the town to another - with cloths, and then bring metal spoons towards it, this could create enough static electricity to create sparks to illuminate the night.

11

CALAMITY COMICS

2

HOW TO MAKE DIAMONDS FROM YOUR PENCILS

THE SCIENCE COMIC YOU NEVER KNEW YOU NEEDED — CHEMISTRY EDITION

Gah! Archie used up all of his pocket money at the weekend, but there are fresh doughnuts at the bakery and Archie loves a jam-filled one . . .

The queue is out of the door, but if Archie joins now he'll be guaranteed a doughnut.

But he's short on money . . .

Archie just has his school bag and packed lunch. How can he pay?

Can you help? Should Archie . . .

A) ASK NICELY FOR A FREE DOUGHNUT?

B) GRAB HIS PENCIL CASE?

C) FORGET ABOUT THE DOUGHNUT?

If you chose **A**, then sadly this doesn't work because his aunt owns the bakery and she's cross with Archie after he broke her favourite vase.

If you chose **B**, WELL DONE! Archie can use what's inside his pencil case to make some money.

If you chose **C**, then Archie has a miserable time eating his soggy sandwiches whilst dreaming of a freshly baked doughnut.

WHAT'S THE SCIENCE?

OK, OK, so your pencil case is likely to reveal a bunch of pencils and a ruler, rather than a money maker. But there are diamonds in there . . . sort of!

Diamonds and graphite (the grey stuff running down the middle of pencils) are both made of carbon atoms. The reason you're not writing with diamond-tipped pencils is because of how the carbon atoms are arranged.

In graphite, the carbon atoms peel away from one another easily, and that's why it can make marks on paper. But in diamonds, the carbon atoms are locked together super tight, which is why diamonds are very strong and not useful for writing!

However, it's possible to turn graphite into diamonds using pressure and heat. Ready to try some pressure experiments?

COLLAPSE A BOTTLE

Crush a bottle with air! Heating air in a bottle causes the air inside to expand. When the lid is put on and this air cools, the air pressure inside the bottle decreases and the higher air pressure in the room pushes against the bottle, which causes it to collapse.

You will need:

- A plastic bottle with a cap (experiment with different bottle sizes and shapes)
- A bowl of hot (not boiling) water from the tap*
- A bowl of cold water

*Be careful – ask an adult for help.

Instructions:

1. Take the cap off. Then ask an adult to help put the bottle into the bowl of hot water. Don't let water go inside the bottle.

2. After 30 seconds, ask an adult to help you screw on the cap. Then remove the bottle from the bowl.

3. Dunk the bottle into the bowl of cold water for a few seconds.

4. Watch the bottle collapse!

EGG IN A BOTTLE

Get a whole hard-boiled egg into a bottle! When the air cools inside the bottle, the higher outside air pressure pushes in the egg. To get it out, ask an adult to turn the bottle upside down and blow into it (to increase the air pressure in the bottle).

You will need:

- A glass jar or bottle (with an opening a little smaller than the egg)
- A bowl of hot (not boiling) water from the tap**
- One peeled, hard-boiled egg (or small blown-up balloon)
- A bowl of cold water with ice cubes***

**Be careful – ask an adult for help.
***Don't touch ice with bare hands as it can cause injury from ice burns.

Instructions:

1. Place the bottle or jar in the bowl containing hot water.

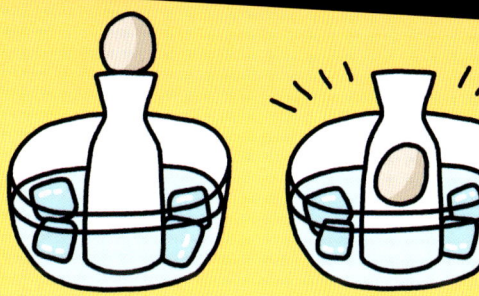

2. Place the egg on top of the bottle, and then move these to the bowl containing cold water and ice cubes. Watch the egg get sucked in!

To turn his pencils into diamonds, Archie would need to place the graphite under intense pressure (about 50,000 times the pressure on Earth's surface) and an extremely high temperature (a whopping 1,600°C!) – so that the atoms could rearrange themselves from their flaky formation into one that was close and tight. Science could help Archie become a millionaire! If only he had a chamber that could create such a high pressure and temperature . . .

CALAMITY COMICS

HOW TO SURVIVE AT SEA AS A NEW PIRATE

THE SCIENCE COMIC YOU NEVER KNEW YOU NEEDED — **CHEMISTRY EDITION**

Granny has joined Captain Rottenleg's crew of scurvy pirates. She's in charge of spotting sea monsters and making the meals. However, the ship doesn't have any salt to sprinkle on their chips because Granny forgot to bring it . . .

The pirate crew is getting hungry. It's hard work being a pirate!

And Captain Rottenleg was looking forward to salted chips with his fish.

Granny needs to come up with a plan . . .

. . . before they feed her to a sea monster!

Should pirate Granny . . .

A) GRAB A BUCKET OF SEA WATER?

B) DISTRACT THEM WITH A SEA SHANTY?

C) HIDE?

If you chose A, this is a GOOD idea! Granny can make salt crystals. If you chose B, oh dear! Granny's sea shanty, whilst fun to sing, sends her to the pirates' slide because Rottenleg STILL hasn't got salted chips. If you chose C, eek! It doesn't take long for them to find Granny and throw her overboard to a sea monster!

WHAT'S THE SCIENCE?

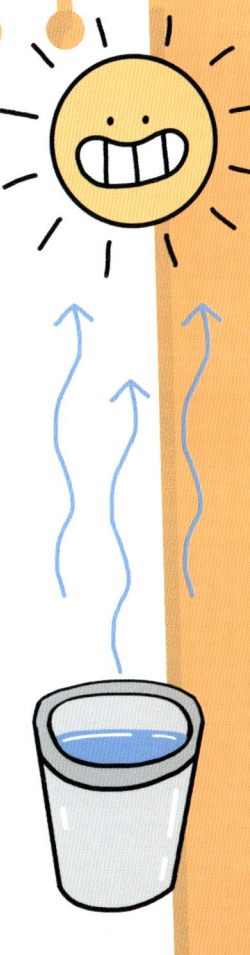

Evaporation is going to help Granny. This is a clever process that turns a **liquid** into a **gas**. When **molecules** of water (a liquid) are heated, they get more energy and move faster, which causes the molecules to spread out. When they spread out enough to escape the pull of the loose bonds that hold the molecules together as a liquid, they then become an invisible vapour or gas. This process is called evaporation.

Water boils at 100°C, but the surface of water can evaporate at a lower temperature if wind or sunshine gives the surface molecules enough energy to break free from the bonds. Salt doesn't melt at this temperature, so it is left behind as the water evaporates. Once the water has gone and only salt is left, the salt forms **crystals** (a process called crystallisation).

Let's make some crystals and see this science in action.

MAKE YOUR OWN SALT CRYSTALS

You'll see how evaporation and crystals are formed in real time and have a very cool ornament too!

You will need:

- A pan*
- 100ml cold water
- 40g salt
- A tablespoon
- A wooden spoon
- A jar
- A lolly stick or chopstick
- Cotton thread

*Be careful – ask an adult for help when heating up the water.

This is a similar method that is used to get the sea salt that can be sprinkled on food (but on a much smaller scale!).

Instructions:

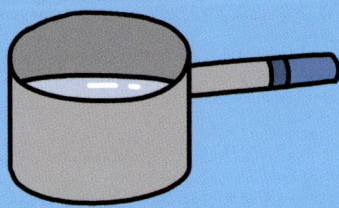 

1. Place the water in a pan and ask an adult to bring it gently to the boil.

2. With an adult, add the salt gradually (about one tablespoon at a time). Stir until all the salt dissolves.

3. Turn off the heat and let the mixture cool in the pan.

4. When cool, pour into a jar.

5. Tie the cotton thread to the lolly stick or chopstick. Then hang the stick over the jar so the cotton is in the salt solution.

6. Leave it for about a week! You will see salt crystals on the string.

If Granny leaves a shallow tray of seawater on the deck, then the heat from the Sun could evaporate the water, leaving behind salt crystals. It might take a couple of weeks for these to form though, so she could try to distract the pirates with one of her epic hip-hop routines whilst they wait OR she could get salt crystals in a few minutes by boiling the salt water in a pan.

CALAMITY COMICS

HOW TO GET CABBAGE OFF THE SCHOOL MENU

THE SCIENCE COMIC YOU NEVER KNEW YOU NEEDED — **CHEMISTRY EDITION**

It's Wednesday and that means only one thing: it's red cabbage for school dinners. Nobody minds the cabbage sandwiches and cabbage bake, but the aftermath of Cabbage Day is that Mrs Trumpton fills the classroom with cabbage farts . . .

Mo is supposed to be sitting at the front of the class after lunch.

And, unsurprisingly, nobody wants to swap seats with him!

Mo's got until lunch time to come up with a plan . . .

Or he's going to be in the line of fire all afternoon!

Should Mo . . .

A) ASK HIS MUM TO PICK HIM UP EARLY?

B) STICK A PEG ON HIS NOSE?

C) GET BICARBONATE OF SODA FROM THE KITCHEN?

If you chose A, unfortunately, Mo's mum refused to pick him up and now he's in for hours of whiffy teacher farts.

If you chose B, this works for a while but the peg is painful and farts seep in through the badly fitting nose clamp. Bleurgh!

If you chose C, this is GREAT. Mo can use it to get cabbage off the menu.

WHAT'S THE SCIENCE?

The pH scale is going to be helpful. A **pH indicator**, such as litmus paper, can be used as a colourful way to tell us how acidic things are. The redder the indicator turns, the more acidic something is; the bluer, the more alkaline. This can be a handy tool for scientists to identify a chemical, for example. **Acids** and **alkalis** are everywhere. You've probably eaten acidic things, such as lemons. Alkalis are things such as soaps - hopefully you haven't eaten those!

And guess what? Red cabbage can be a pH indicator because it contains **anthocyanin**. The pH chart for a red-cabbage indicator is different. It turns red or pink for acids, violet for neutrals (e.g. water), and blue, green or yellow for alkalis.

Let's mess with the colour of a cabbage using **bicarbonate of soda** to see how this can help Mo!

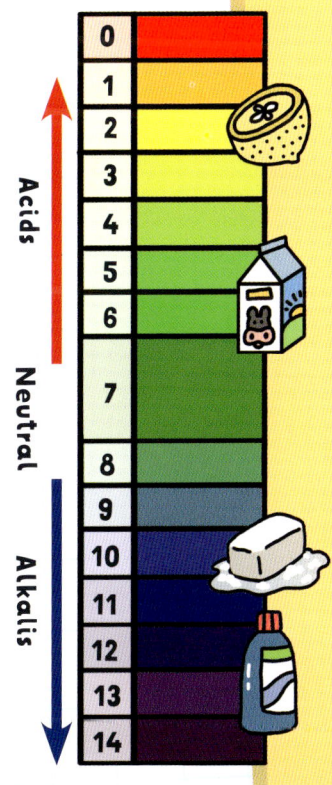

21

MAKE A PH INDICATOR SOLUTION

Have a go at looking at how acidic things are by mixing the water from a boiled red cabbage with different things in your kitchen.

Try experimenting with other ingredients, such as lemonade, soap and different fruit juices.

You will need:

- A quarter of red cabbage
- A chopping board
- A sharp knife*
- Two heatproof jugs
- Boiling water*
- A colander
- Three glasses
- One tablespoon each of fruit juice, white vinegar and bicarbonate of soda
- Three tablespoons

*Be careful – ask an adult for help.

Instructions:

1. Ask an adult to help cut up the red cabbage into small pieces. Red cabbage can stain so protect clothes and surfaces.

2. Put the cabbage in the jug and then ask an adult to cover the cabbage with boiling water. Leave for about ten minutes.

3. Ask an adult to pour the cabbage water through the colander into another jug. Let this cool.

4. When cool, pour into each glass.

fruit juice

white vinegar

bicarbonate of soda

5. Add a different ingredient to each glass and give it a stir to see what colour the water turns.

The cabbage water will turn red or pink for acids, and blue, green or yellow for alkalis. Try blowing on the cabbage water – you might see it turn red because of the carbon dioxide in breath mixing with the water to make a weak acid.

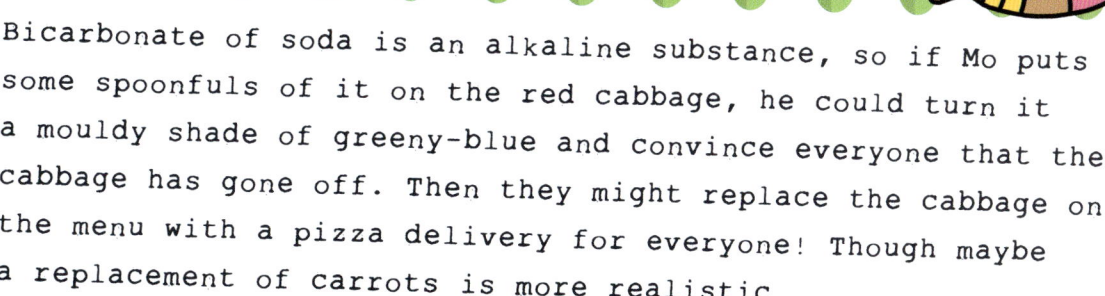

Bicarbonate of soda is an alkaline substance, so if Mo puts some spoonfuls of it on the red cabbage, he could turn it a mouldy shade of greeny-blue and convince everyone that the cabbage has gone off. Then they might replace the cabbage on the menu with a pizza delivery for everyone! Though maybe a replacement of carrots is more realistic . . .

CALAMITY COMICS

HOW TO MAKE THE MAGIC SHOW SPARKLE

5

THE SCIENCE COMIC YOU NEVER KNEW YOU NEEDED — CHEMISTRY EDITION

Ava is visiting her uncle Bertie, in New York, US. He's putting on a big magic show at the Statue of Liberty, but he's lost his wand and with that, his confidence . . .

Ava needs to help Bertie put on the best show of all time . . .

Because The Great Zamboni-Stalloney, Bertie's hero, is in the crowd.

So how can Ava create the biggest trick New York has ever seen . . .

. . . and help her uncle fulfil his dream of impressing The Great Zamboni-Stalloney?

Should Ava . . .

A) PANIC?

B) TRY A CARD TRICK?

C) GRAB SOME VINEGAR AND SALT?

If you chose A, No! Panicking is never the best option when science can help!
If you chose B, then Ava does her best but can't remember how to do the trick, so the crowd start booing and The Great Zamboni-Stalloney leaves.
If you chose C, FANTASTIC choice! Ava uses science to make the statue shine.

WHAT'S THE SCIENCE?

Copper and chemical reactions will help Ava. Did you know that the Statue of Liberty is made of different metals, including a copper coating? When copper is exposed to different chemicals, it changes colour. The statue was originally a reddish-brown colour. Then the copper reacted with **oxygen** in the air to make copper oxide (a reaction called **oxidation**) on the outside of the statue. The copper oxide then reacted in different ways with other chemicals in the air (mostly from pollution from the city nearby and from sea spray), to create the blue-green colour we see today.

Adding vinegar and salt to copper oxide causes another reaction - it dissolves the copper oxide, due to acid in the vinegar.

Let's have a go at our own copper chemistry experiment to see how Ava's 'trick' works.

Statue of Liberty

MAKE YOUR PENNIES SHINE OR TURN GREEN

When copper reacts with different chemicals, it changes colour. Let's experiment!

You will need:

- A bowl (not a metal one)
- One teaspoon of salt
- 50ml white vinegar
- A wooden spoon
- Two copper coins (1p or 2p coins)
- A dry cloth

Instructions:

1. Add the salt to your bowl.

2. Add the vinegar to the salt and stir until all the salt disappears.

3. Place the coins in the solution for about five minutes.

4. Now take them out and give them a quick wipe with the dry cloth. Look how shiny they are!

Want to turn the copper coins blue-green? Then after step three, take the coins out and leave them wet with the solution on for about 24 hours. This will help them to oxidise and form a compound called verdigris.

If Ava uses salt and vinegar to clean the surface of the copper (by dissolving the copper oxide) on the Statue of Liberty, it will change colour from green to orange AND look super shiny. How could this not impress The Great Zamboni-Stalloney? Hurray for Ava saving the day and her uncle's magic show. Of course, it's not really magic . . .

CALAMITY COMICS
HOW TO RESCUE YOUR FRIEND'S PARTY

6

THE SCIENCE COMIC YOU NEVER KNEW YOU NEEDED — CHEMISTRY EDITION

What should have been the most perfect birthday celebration for Zoe's friend, Aria, is now about to become a disaster...

Zoe is in charge of the chocolate fountain...

But she soon discovers there's a hole in it!

Now there's liquid chocolate everywhere...

And the chocolate river is getting closer and closer to Aria...

Should Zoe . . .

A) TELL ARIA TO CANCEL HER PARTY?

B) START MOPPING?

C) TURN THE AIR CONDITIONING ON?

If you chose A, Aria is devastated! And her party dress is chocolate brown!

If you chose B, Zoe is still mopping when the party guests arrive and now the hall is a chocolate slip 'n' slide.

If you chose C, AWESOME CHOICE! This will quickly stop the choco-disaster.

WHAT'S THE SCIENCE?

Everything around us is in one of three states: a **solid**, a liquid or a gas. Shoes? A solid! Water in a puddle? A liquid! Bubbles in a fizzy drink? A gas (**carbon dioxide**)!

It's possible to change the state of some things by heating them, such as water to water vapour (it changes from a liquid to a gas). And it's possible to change some states by cooling them, for example water to ice (it changes from a liquid to a solid). And this is the science that is going to help Zoe!

Let's have a go at changing the state of chocolate. Yum!

MAKE CHOCOLATE CRISPY TREATS

Using heat, we can look at how chocolate changes from a solid state to a liquid state. And then we can see it change back to a solid state.

You will need:

- 100g chocolate chips
- One small sandwich bag
- A bowl of warm tap water (up to 50°C)
- 30g rice pops or cornflakes
- A spoon

Instructions:

1. Place the chocolate in the bag.

2. Gently place the bag of chocolate in the bowl of warm water.

3. Watch carefully. You will see over the next five or so minutes that the chocolate will start to melt – turning from a solid state to a liquid state.

4. Once the chocolate is fully liquid, remove the bag from the water and pour the cereal into the bag. Stir to mix.

5. Place the bag in the fridge and leave for about 30 minutes.

6. Take the bag out of the fridge – the chocolate will now be a solid again because it has cooled. Turn the bag inside out to get your yummy treat!

Switching off the chocolate fountain and turning on the venue's air conditioning will cool the chocolate quickly – turning it from a runny, uncontrollable liquid into its solid state. This will make clearing up the chocolate a breeze. And any chocolate that didn't hit the floor can be packaged up into yummy party treats. Hurray for chocolate parties!

CALAMITY COMICS

HOW TO GET ACROSS QUICKSAND

7

THE SCIENCE COMIC YOU NEVER KNEW YOU NEEDED — CHEMISTRY EDITION

On the way back from a school trip, Zoe's class stops for a break. They take a stroll after a picnic lunch, but unfortunately, they find themselves faced with quicksand along a stretch of riverbank.

Ishaan doesn't think it's quicksand, so he chucks his backpack in to check . . .

And everyone watches as it slowly sinks!

It's definitely quicksand and it's blocking their way back to the bus stop . . .

And walking the long way round means a trek through some very thorny bushes!

Should Zoe and her class . . .

A) RUN ACROSS THE QUICKSAND?

B) WALK SLOWLY ACROSS THE QUICKSAND?

C) TAKE THE THORNY ROUTE HOME?

If you chose A, this is better than walking slowly. If they run over quicksand quickly, it *should* stay solid. But C is safer! If you chose B, uh oh! If they go slow, they'll sink - like Ishaan's backpack. If you chose C, this is the best option. Sure, they get scratched and miss the bus, but getting stuck in quicksand could be very dangerous.

WHAT'S THE SCIENCE?

Quicksand is a mixture of sand and water. Does that make it a liquid or a solid? Well, it's a bit of both! It might look like a solid, but if you gently stand on it, it behaves like a liquid. This is why you can sink in quicksand. And the special term for a fluid that doesn't follow the regular rules of flow for liquids is **non-Newtonian fluid**.

When force is applied to a non-Newtonian fluid, the way it flows (also known as its **viscosity**) changes. Guess what else is a non-Newtonian fluid? Ketchup! Applying a force by giving the ketchup a shake, changes the flow and it becomes runnier.

Want to have a go at making a non-Newtonian fluid? Then just turn the page . . .

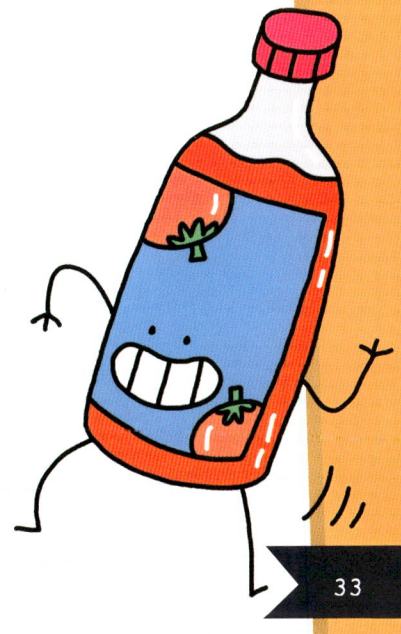

MAKE OOBLECK

Oobleck works like quicksand, so this is a safer way to see how quicksand acts when you add pressure to it – without having to throw your backpack in actual quicksand!

If you added 3.5kg of cornflour and 1-2 litres of water to a 15-litre tray, then you could try running on it! Don't forget to protect the floor, though. If you sink in the oobleck, use your hand to make a hole next to your foot to release it. Keep the oobleck tray away from small children and animals, so they don't get stuck.

You will need:

- A bowl
- 320g cornflour
- 235ml water
- A spoon

Instructions:

1. Put your cornflour into the bowl.

2. Add the water.

3. Stir the cornflour and water together until fully combined.

4. You'll know the oobleck is fully mixed when you can squish a handful of it into a ball and then it oozes back into a liquid when you release the pressure, and there is no dry cornflour left.

5. Have fun playing with it!

Pssst! It's very important you don't wash oobleck down the sink, as it can clog drains. Put the oobleck in the compost bin when you've finished with it.

So, in theory, if Zoe's class ran across the quicksand, this should keep it in a solid enough state to give them enough time to escape before it swallows them up. BUT, in real life, it's always best to turn back and avoid quicksand, as it may be runnier than you expect.

CALAMITY COMICS

HOW TO CARRY A DINOSAUR EGG ACROSS A JUNGLE

8

THE SCIENCE COMIC YOU NEVER KNEW YOU NEEDED — **CHEMISTRY EDITION**

What's this?! Anika has discovered an actual dinosaur egg whilst on an expedition with her volcanologist mum in the jungle. They want to keep it safe and get it as far away from the ready-to-explode volcano as possible . . .

But it's tricky carrying a dinosaur egg as it's pretty big and slippery . . .

And they only have the essentials for their hike with them.

So how can they get the egg across the jungle . . .

. . . without breaking it?

Should Anika . . .

A) RUN REALLY FAST WITH THE EGG?

B) USE THEIR MILK AND VINEGAR?

C) LEAVE THE EGG BEHIND?

If you chose **A**, Anika drops the heavy, slippery egg, leaving a trail of dino egg goop behind and losing the greatest discovery of her time.

If you chose **B**, WELL DONE! Science can help Anika carry the egg.

If you chose **C**, then the lava will soon hard-boil the egg.

WHAT'S THE SCIENCE?

Cow's milk contains molecules called **casein**. When this is heated and combined with an acid, such as vinegar, the casein molecules move around and form new long chains (called **polymers**). In this changed form, the 'milk' can be moulded, a bit like playdough, and it acts like plastic! Yup! You read that right. You can make plastic out of milk!

This substance is called casein plastic. Before 1945, milk was often turned into this plastic to create buttons, pens and combs. It was even used to make jewellery for Queen Mary of England!

How can this plastic help Anika? Let's give the science a go and then find out . . .

MAKE YOUR OWN PLASTIC

I know this seems like it will never work, but it does! Have a go at making plastic with some ingredients from your kitchen. Just remember to throw any milk plastic in the bin when you have finished with it – don't throw it down the sink.

You will need:

- A microwaveable bowl*
- 235ml cow's milk
- A spoon
- Four tablespoons of white vinegar
- A sieve
- Paper towels
- Biscuit cutters (optional)

*Be careful – ask an adult for help when using the microwave.

Repeat with different acids, such as lemon juice, to see if it makes a change to the plastic.

Instructions:

1. Pour the milk into the bowl and ask an adult to help heat it in the microwave for about one and a half minutes. The milk should be hot but not bubbling.

2. Pour the vinegar into the hot milk. Then ask an adult to help stir it for about one minute. You should see the milk starting to clump.

3. Gently put the milk in the sieve to strain it. Push down on the clumps with the back of the spoon to remove the liquid.

4. Bring the clumps together, rinse and then dry with a paper towel.

5. Now you can shape it! Use your hands or biscuit cutters. It will then take two to three days to completely harden.

Try solving Anika's dilemma on a smaller scale by creating a plastic case and handle for a chicken's egg.

If Anika uses the milk in her flask and the vinegar she packed for her salad dressing, she could create a plastic case and handle to make it easier to carry the egg across the jungle and away from the volcano. Okay, so Anika would need A LOT of milk and vinegar to make the plastic big enough, but it could work! And then Anika could adopt the dinosaur, name him Morris and look after him as he grows up to be a full-size Stegosaurus.

CALAMITY COMICS

HOW TO WIN THE SCIENCE FAIR

9

THE SCIENCE COMIC YOU NEVER KNEW YOU NEEDED — **CHEMISTRY EDITION**

Rocky and Flynn have just heard that there is a prize for the best project at the Science Fair, and they really want to win it . . .

But what makes a prize-winning science project?

Maybe they need some inspiration from a scientist?

Surely US chemist Dr Harry Coover knew what he was doing when trying to create a special clear plastic?

Or did he? It turns out he accidentally created Super Glue instead!

So what makes a great science project . . .

A) MAKING MISTAKES?

B) EXPERIMENTING?

C) HAVING FUN?

If you chose A, B or C, then WELL DONE! Science is all about trying new things, having fun and making mistakes — I like to think of them as 'learnings' rather than mistakes!

WHAT'S THE SCIENCE?

Did you know that many brilliant inventions were created by accident? For example, in 1943, when chemist James Wright was trying to create a new, cheap rubber, he added boric acid into silicone oil, which formed a putty. He accidentally discovered it was bouncy when it dropped on the floor!

But it was Peter Hodgson who thought this would make a fun toy (later named Silly Putty). More than 300 million plastic eggs with Silly Putty in have been sold worldwide since! A slimier version can be created at home using PVA glue.

Long, strand-like chains in the glue (called polymers) slide past each other easily. BUT when mixed with a 'slime activator', a chemical reaction causes the molecules to change position and become tangled (a bit like a bowl of spaghetti). The result is gloopy, stringy slime! Want to make some of your own?

CREATE YOUR OWN SLIME

Here's an easy slime EXPERIMENT - use different colours, eco glitter or glow-in-the-dark paint to jazz it up. Have FUN making it and then playing with it! And don't worry about making MISTAKES.

You will need:

- A mixing bowl
- 200ml **PVA glue***
- Liquid food colouring, glow-in-the-dark paint, eco glitter (optional)
- A spoon
- One teaspoon of bicarbonate of soda
- Two tablespoons of saline solution (a contact lens solution containing boric acid)*
- An airtight container

*Ask an adult for help when using this.

Instructions:

1. Add the glue into a mixing bowl. Stir in a few drops of food colouring (add more for a darker colour) or paint, and/or sprinkle of glitter now if you're using it.

2. Add the bicarbonate of soda and stir until smooth.

3. Add in the saline solution and then stir slowly.

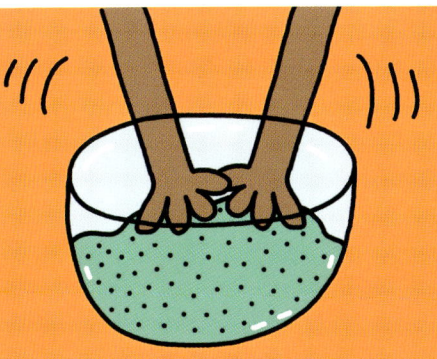

4. Use your hands to knead it for five–ten minutes. The mixture will start to come together and become stringy, like slime.

5. Play and have fun! Just don't forget to protect surfaces and your clothes, as it can get messy!

To keep your slime fresh, store it in an airtight container after play. It should last for weeks!

German chemist Dr Fritz Klatte (1880–1934) discovered PVA glue in 1912 when he created a reaction between acetylene and acetic acid, and identified the long-chain polymers that make PVA glue.

If Rocky and Flynn make slime using PVA glue, bicarbonate of soda, and saline solution as their 'slime activator', they have a great chance of winning the trophy – especially if they explain the chemistry behind their creation. They don't mind if they don't win though, because they had such a good time making, stretching and squishing the slime, and experimenting with different colours.

CALAMITY COMICS

HOW TO SEND A SECRET MESSAGE

10

THE SCIENCE COMIC YOU NEVER KNEW YOU NEEDED — CHEMISTRY EDITION

Archie and his grandad are both in time-out for pranking Dad by leaving a gigantic toy spider in the bath. But Grandad has just thought of a funny joke he desperately needs to tell Archie . . .

"Shriek!"

Archie's mum is not happy. It's taking ages to calm down Dad after he had the fright of his life . . .

Grandad wants to write down the joke and pass it to Archie . . .

"Hee, Hee, Hee!"

But if Mum sees Grandad still being silly, he might not get ice cream after dinner . . .

So how can Grandad get his joke to Archie without Mum reading it?

Should Grandad . . .

A) DISTRACT MUM AND THROW IT OVER?

B) GRAB A LEMON?

C) HOPE ARCHIE CAN READ HIS MIND?

If you chose A, bad idea. The note lands on Archie's mum's head and she opens it up to reveal the joke. No ice cream for Grandad!

If you chose B, WELL DONE! it's perfect for writing a secret note.

If you chose C, Archie has no idea what Grandad was trying to tell him. He needs to use real science to get a message to Archie!

WHAT'S THE SCIENCE?

If you squeeze a cut lemon, you'll see a liquid run from the fruit. And this is what Archie's grandad needs to write his secret message.

On paper, the lemon juice doesn't show. Now, that's not so useful if you want someone to be able to read what you've written with it. But fear not, here's the clever bit: if you place the paper next to a heat source, this creates a chemical reaction that makes the words turn brown. Why? Well, the lemon juice breaks down, which releases carbon. The carbon reacts with the oxygen in the air. This process is called oxidation.

Want to try the science?

WRITE A SECRET MESSAGE

Time to master the art of sending secret messages just like a top-secret agent.

You will need:

- A bowl
- Half a lemon
- A piece of paper
- A small paint brush
- A hairdryer*

*Be careful - ask an adult for help when using this.

Compare this method with using 25g of bicarbonate of soda mixed with 30ml of water to write messages. Reveal this message by brushing with grape juice (a natural pH indicator). The message should appear in a different colour.

Instructions:

1. Squeeze the lemon until all the juice is in the bowl.

2. Dip the paint brush into the juice and use it to write a message on the paper.

3. Let the paper dry completely, and you will see your message has disappeared.

4. To see your message again, ask an adult to use a hairdryer to warm the paper.

What fruit is square and purple?

A lemon in disguise!

5. Watch as your message reappears!

So, Grandad needs to write with lemon juice and then he can safely pass his joke to Archie, because Archie's mum will think it is just a piece of paper! And when she's not looking, Archie can heat the paper and see what Grandad has been itching to tell him.

CALAMITY COMICS

HOW TO WIN A SCHOOL COMPETITION

11

THE SCIENCE COMIC YOU NEVER KNEW YOU NEEDED — **CHEMISTRY EDITION**

Wei's class are trying to work out who can launch a paper aeroplane the furthest and Wei wants to win . . .

Wei has seen everyone make their paper planes . . .

Tweaking the folds in the paper, using different origami techniques . . .

And chucking them across the school field.

So what can Wei do to get his plane to go further?

Should Wei . . .

A) TAKE A RUN UP?

B) THROW THE PLANE WHILST ON A TRAMPOLINE?

C) GRAB A BOTTLE OF FIZZY POP?

If you chose A, this could work! However, the rest of Wei's class see this and take a run up too.

If you chose B, this would help it Wei timed the jump and launch well, but there aren't any trampolines at school!

If you chose C, EXCELLENT IDEA. A chemical reaction will give it a boost!

WHAT'S THE SCIENCE?

Fizzy drinks are packed with a gas called carbon dioxide. The carbon dioxide molecules bond with the water molecules, but only under pressure. As soon as you take off the lid, you release the pressure and the bubbles of carbon dioxide come whizzing out.

If you add something to the fizzy drink, such as bicarbonate of soda or mint sweets, this helps break the bonds between the gas and water very, very quickly, because it gives the carbon dioxide gas something else to cling to. The gas bubbles then get larger and shoot out of the bottle, causing an eruption of gas.

Turn over to see the science in action and find out how this can help Wei.

MAKE A ROCKET

Make your own rocket with a bottle of diet cola and a packet of mints. You can also try a bubbly reaction to see carbon dioxide being released using vinegar (200ml) and adding bicarbonate of soda (one tablespoon) or one or two effervescent vitamin C tablets.

You will need:

- An outdoor area*
- A two-litre bottle of diet cola
- A packet of mints, such as Mentos
- One sheet of A4 paper
- Sticky tape

*This can get very messy!

Having the paper tube helps add more mints to the bottle at a time, but an adult could drop mints in by hand.

Instructions:

1. Place the cola bottle on a flat surface outdoors and remove the lid.

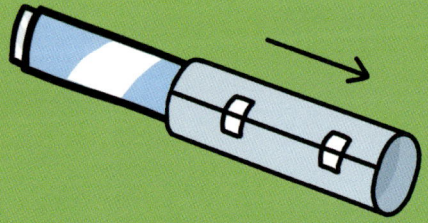

2. Roll the paper around the packet of mints and tape in place. Then slide off the paper tube.

3. Take the mints out of the packet and load them into the tube. Then ask an adult to hold the tube, with their finger over the bottom, over the bottle.

4. Then they should remove their finger, to let the mints slide into the bottle.

5. Stand back and watch the bottle erupt!

Try this with regular cola – does it make a difference? What happens if you use warm or cold cola?

Since there were no rules for the paper plane challenge, if Wei attaches his plane to the top of a massive cola bottle (at least 500 litres!) and a whopper amount of mints or baking soda was added, he could send his plane soaring into the sky, and probably further than any of his classmates' other planes.
Cola rocket for the win!

CALAMITY COMICS

HOW TO BE A DETECTIVE

12

THE SCIENCE COMIC YOU NEVER KNEW YOU NEEDED — CHEMISTRY EDITION

Somebody has drawn a picture of a dinosaur on Mr Trumpton's sheet music – right before singing assembly! Mr Trumpton is not happy, but Amy is on the case. She has three suspects in mind . . .

At 8:18am the headteacher was seen loitering by the piano . . .

At 8:36am the receptionist was seen with ink stains on her top . . .

At 8:54am the caretaker was seen throwing out pens, claiming they had run out of ink . . .

How can Amy know for sure which of these suspects is guilty of the dino graffiti?

Should Amy . . .

A) INTERVIEW EACH SUSPECT?

B) LOOK AT THE INK IN THEIR PENS?

C) STOP ASSEMBLY UNTIL THE CASE IS SOLVED?

If you chose **A**, now Amy's in trouble. The headteacher did not like being interviewed about a crime – not one bit.

If you chose **B**, EXCELLENT. Separating the colours in the inks will help Amy find out who did it!

If you chose **C**, oh dear. Nobody wants singing assembly cancelled. NOBODY! It's the only time everyone can shout their heads off out of tune and get praised for it.

WHAT'S THE SCIENCE?

Chromatography will help Amy solve the case, because it is a brilliant way to separate mixtures. Coloured inks are made of a few different colours (called pigments) that are mixed together. So, if ink is put on a paper towel, the different colour ink molecules will travel at different speeds through the paper towel and separate out into the different colours. The most soluble colours (the ones that mix with water the best) travel further and faster than less soluble colours, which stick to the paper and do not travel. Wetting the paper separates out the colours even further. This is very handy when ink stains look very similar!

Want to try chromatography and see how it can help Amy? Then turn the page!

HAVE A GO AT CHROMATOGRAPHY

This is a fun experiment to look at the different colours that make up one colour in the ink of a pen.

You will need:

- A small bowl
- Water
- Paper towel
- Felt-tip pens that are not permanent or washable*
- A chopstick or a pencil

*Washable pens won't work because they usually contain one type of ink, so you won't see much separation of colour. But you know what? Give it a go and see for yourself!

Your finished piece even has a fancy name: a chromatogram.

Instructions:

1. Pour a little bit of water into the bowl.

2. Draw a row of coloured-in circles at the bottom of the paper towel with each pen you want to test.

3. Roll the paper towel around the pencil to attach it, then hang the paper towel over the bowl, bottom first, so it is just touching the water's surface and watch as the pigments in the ink move up the paper towel.

If Amy uses chromatography on the dinosaur drawing and also on each of the suspects' pens, she will be able to match the ink combinations on the dino graffiti to the ink in one of the pens. And once she matches the pen to its owner - she'll have her culprit! The ink colours all look very similar on the page, but Amy discovers it is the dark blue marker . . .

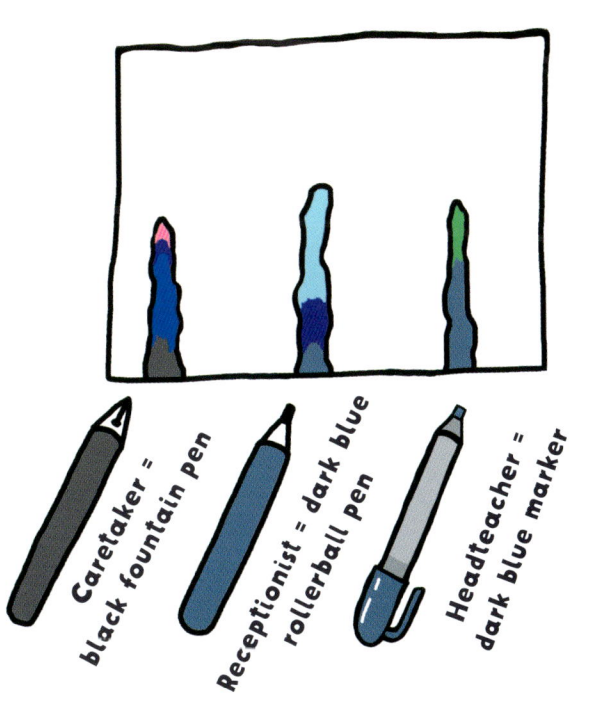

Caretaker = black fountain pen
Receptionist = dark blue rollerball pen
Headteacher = dark blue marker

CALAMITY COMICS

HOW TO MAKE YOUR OWN ICE-CREAM STAND

13

THE SCIENCE COMIC YOU NEVER KNEW YOU NEEDED — CHEMISTRY EDITION

It's the school fair and Mo is in charge of the ice-cream stand. However, his dog Brian loves ice cream and instead of helping Mo set up, he's helped himself to all of the ice-cream tubs for dogs, whilst squashing the rest of the ice cream . . .

The ice-cream stand is the highlight of the fair . . .

And Mo has worked really hard to get his stand ready.

How is Mo going to run his ice-cream stand . . .

. . . when he is completely out of ice cream because of Brian?

Should Mo . . .

A) TELL EVERYONE THE DOG RUINED HIS ICE CREAM?

B) PRETEND TO BE HIS TWIN BROTHER FAAZ?

C) GRAB MILK, SALT AND ICE CUBES?

If you chose A, whilst true, the hungry queue is not sympathetic because Mo has used that excuse a lot for his homework, and they are starting to grow suspicious.

If you chose B, errr, Mo doesn't have a twin and everyone knows it, and now he has people demanding ice cream and getting very cross.

If you chose C, HOORAY! Mo uses science to quickly create more ice cream!

WHAT'S THE SCIENCE?

The science of making ice cream in a bag is all about how salt interacts with ice. Ice alone is not cold enough to harden milk into ice cream, but when salt is added to ice it forces the ice to melt. To melt, the ice needs to take heat from what's around it and so the ice-cream ingredients get colder, until they freeze.

And this science makes it possible to create instant ice cream. Talking of ice cream, want to make some?

Heat

MAKE INSTANT ICE CREAM

Here's a brilliant way to make your own ice cream without expensive equipment, and you get to see science in action. To make chocolate or strawberry ice cream, use flavoured milk!

You will need:

- Two sealable sandwich bags: one large and one small
- Ice cubes*
- 125g table salt
- 120ml milk
- One tablespoon of sugar
- Half a teaspoon of vanilla extract
- A tea towel or warm gloves

*Don't touch ice with bare hands as it can cause injury from ice burns.

Try placing ice in a bag to see how it compares in temperature to the ice-salt bag. The ice-salt bag should be colder. Don't forget to wear gloves when touching the ice or bags.

Instructions:

1. Pour the ice and salt into the large bag.

2. Pour the milk, sugar and vanilla extract into the small bag. Squeeze out as much air as possible from the bag and seal it tight, before giving it a shake to mix the ingredients.

3. Place the milk bag inside the ice and salt bag. Make sure the ice surrounds the milk bag and squeeze out the air before sealing it tight.

4. Wrap the bags in a tea towel or put on gloves to protect your hands. Then shake the bags to get everything icy cold.

6. Enjoy!

5. Keep jiggling and squishing until the ice cream is the consistency you like. Five minutes usually does it.

Can you make ice cream freeze faster? Experiment with the amount of salt, type of salt and how much you shake the mixture.

So, with milk from the tea stand, a couple of sandwich bags from the cake stand and some salt from the popcorn stand, Mo would be able to make ice cream, thanks to the magic of science! Though it would definitely taste better if Mo added some vanilla essence!

GLOSSARY

ACID: A substance that has a pH value lower than seven.

ALKALI: A substance that has a pH value higher than seven.

ANTHOCYANIN: A chemical found in red, blue or purple fruit and vegetables that can tell us whether something is acidic or not.

ATOMS: The tiny building blocks that make up everything in the Universe.

BICARBONATE OF SODA: An alkaline powder used in baking.

CARBON DIOXIDE: A gas made of carbon and oxygen atoms.

CASEIN: A protein in milk.

CHROMATOGRAPHY: A way of separating mixtures of colours.

CRYSTALS: A solid where its atoms sit in a specific pattern.

ELECTRONS: Negatively charged parts of an atom.

EVAPORATION: The process where a liquid changes to a gas.

GAS: One of the three states that a substance can be. Steam is a gas.

LIQUID: One of the three states that a substance can be. Water is a liquid.

MOLECULES: Two or more atoms bonded together.

NEUTRONS: Parts of an atom with no charge.

NON-NEWTONIAN FLUID: A fluid that doesn't follow the normal rules of liquids.

OXIDATION: When a substance interacts with oxygen.

OXYGEN: A gas found in air.

PH INDICATOR: Something that can show if a substance is an acid or an alkali.

POLYMERS: Long chains of molecules that are bonded together.

PROTONS: Positively charged parts of an atom.

SOLID: One of the three states that a substance can be. Ice is a solid.

STATIC ELECTRICITY: An electrical charge that builds up on the surface of an object.

VISCOSITY: How fast or slow a liquid can flow.

INDEX

A
acids 21, 23, 25, 37, 38, 41, 42, 43, 60
alkali 21, 23, 60
anthocyanin 21, 60
atoms 9, 13, 15, 60

C
carbon 13, 45
carbon dioxide 23, 29, 49, 50, 60
casein plastic 37, 38-39
chemical 10, 21, 25, 26
  reactions 25, 41, 43, 45, 50
chromatography 53, 54-55, 60
Coover, Dr Harry 40
copper 25, 26, 27
copper oxide 25, 27
crystals 17, 18-19, 60

E
electrons 9, 10, 11, 60
evaporation 17, 18, 19, 60

G
gas 17, 29, 49, 60

H
Hodgson, Peter 41

K
Klatte, Dr Fritz 43
Kwolek, Stephanie 6

L
liquids (state) 17, 29, 30, 31, 33, 60

M
molecules 17, 37, 41, 49, 53, 60

N
neutrons 9, 60
non-Newtonian fluids 33, 60

O
oobleck 34-35
oxidation 25, 45, 60
oxygen 25, 45, 60

P
pH indicator 21, 22-23, 46, 60
polymers 37, 41, 43
pressure 13, 14-15, 34, 35
protons 9, 60

S
slime 41, 42-43
solids 29, 30, 31, 33, 60
static electricity 9, 10-11, 60

T
Thales 9

V
verdigris 27
viscosity 33, 60

W
Wright, James 41